Disturbing the Buddha

Disturbing the Buddha
Barry Dempster

Brick Books

Library and Archives Canada Cataloguing in Publication

Dempster, Barry, 1952-, author
   Disturbing the Buddha / Barry Dempster.

Poems.
Issued in print and electronic formats.
ISBN 978-1-77131-434-3 (paperback).--ISBN 978-1-77131-435-0 (pdf).--
ISBN 978-1-77131-436-7 (epub)

   I. Title.

PS8557.E4827D58 2016   C811'.54   C2015-907887-3
                                         C2015-907888-1

Copyright © Barry Dempster, 2016

We acknowledge the Canada Council for the Arts, the Government of Canada through the Canada Book Fund, and the Ontario Arts Council for their support of our publishing program.

The author photo was taken by Karen Dempster.
The book is set in Dante.
The cover image is a painting by Barbara Cole called *Three by Four*.
Design and layout by Marijke Friesen.
Printed and bound by Sunville Printco Inc.

Brick Books
431 Boler Road, Box 20081
London, Ontario N6K 4G6

www.brickbooks.ca

CONTENTS

Centre of Attention

    A Circle of White Deck Chairs   /3
    Toy Box   /5
    The Word of God   /7
    The Explained World   /8
    The Walk Home   /9
    As Close as Distance   /10
    Be Drunk   /11
    Tampering   /12
    The ABCs   /13
    Mensch   /15
    Colour Samples   /16
    Our Lives and Nothing Less   /18
    As They Pour the Thirteenth Floor   /20
    The Turtles Practice Finitism   /21

Ten Thousand Repetitions

A Minor Accomplishment

    Toy Box 2: Princess   /33
    Love – after Beatrix Potter   /35
    Six Toasts to Neglected Body Parts   /37
    Portrait of Aphrodite   /40
    The Back Seat   /42
    Swallows   /43
    Rundle Lounge   /44
    Full of Flame   /45
    The Widow   /46
    Whiteouts   /47
    Spider   /48
    Love's Body   /49

Death Notices

    Rothko /53
    Mother Ash /54
    Dangling /57
    Death Notices /58
        1/ Sweet Drowning – after Yeats /58
        2/ Sweet Revenge – after Plath /59
        3/ Sweet Transformation – after Whitman /60
        4/ Sweet Oblivion – after Sexton /61
    Positivity /62
    Milton's Grave /62
    Slaughter /65
    White Pansy, 1927 – Georgia O'Keeffe /66
    Postcard from Lorca, August 1936 /67
    McMichael Gallery, After Hours /68
    Amy Winehouse /69
    The Weeping Monkey – after Julie Oakes /70

Disturbing The Buddha

    1/ Psalm 19 /73
    2/ Lao-tzu /74
    3/ Seng-ts'an /75
    4/ Kūkai /76
    5/ Wu-men /77
    6/ Rumi /78
    7/ Mechthild of Magdeburg /79
    8/ Kabir /80
    9/ Gensei /81
    10/ Ryōkan /82

Acknowledgements /85
Biographical Note /87

For Karen, as always.

Centre of Attention

A CIRCLE OF WHITE DECK CHAIRS

The bar looks out on a circle
of white deck chairs like a Fitzgerald novel
waiting for its characters. My white wine –
crisp Pinot – tastes like a mouthful of silver.
The tablecloth is whiter than the chairs.
And the napkins have pink orchids dabbed
across the linen. So this is the way the indolent
spend the lateness of their afternoons, sipping
the view, painting the air white as a turtle's egg.
Too hot to sit outside, otherwise
I'd fill the lawn with the hum of my breath,
quietly playing centre of attention.

In my story, a lone priest sits at a white
wrought iron table, writing in a notebook
with sin-black covers. He's the only
person in the garden and is therefore bold.
He lets the breeze comb through his wiry grey hair.
The plan is to describe a world of pure spirit
before flesh stirs its shadow cells.
He doesn't know he's being watched by
someone who is making up his every move.
Alone with God, in spite of God, he's not sure which.
His wine tastes like amber beads in a rosary.
He's careful not to swallow his words, spills them
on a blank page, spelling out the various ways
a man will work a common day into chance and fancy.

It wouldn't be worth the effort it takes
to leap a metaphor if I didn't create
a woman for both the priest and me
to puzzle over. Manipulator that I am,
I raise the heat, the late afternoon sun pink
as a plate of smoked salmon. What else can
she do but crumple her paleness into one
of those empty chairs, dangle her fingers
over the almost-burning grass. She is weak
with having just been imagined, hasn't yet
had the opportunity of wrinkles or
rumours or too much to drink. In fact, the bar
doesn't even exist anymore. And the priest
has disappeared into his immaculate
intentions. All that's left is a deck chair,
and the shadow of a story hovering over the white wood.

TOY BOX

These are not my toys
but distractions for my niece and nephew,

fantasies we can share. Lukas is partial
to the stove-white speedboat, pursing

his lips into *vrooms*. Kora prefers
the motley Barbies, a chorus line

of bleached-grass hair and evening gowns
ripped in cool places. Together, we play

Barbie Goes Water Skiing, high heels and all,
until Lukas rams the boat into the wall,

mimicking tremendous explosions, bits
of Barbie cooked mid-air. Of course

Kora fumes, knowing full well
life isn't meant to be that dramatic.

She gathers up the dolls and starts
a game of Fashion Show.

The rest of the afternoon
is trashed. *They're supposed to be dead!*

Lukas screams, kicking in the direction
of Kora, who refuses to relinquish

even one blonde strand of hair.
If I had a choice, the boat

would slide on the ceramic tiles
as if upon a secret lake, and the Barbies

would swim around it like beautiful,
placid sharks. *Let's play Castaway*, I blurt.

Lukas looks as if my eyes just
squirted blood. Kora ignores us both,

bending the Barbies into Russian gymnasts.
No chance of world peace, not here

in this toy box. Could this be why
God left the planet? The deadly boat

floats toward me with a plastic sneer,
Barbies behind me like dolled-up Satans.

The perfect place for a sacrifice: won't be long
before they're playing Obliterate the Uncle.

I am not a toy, I try to say
before remembering toys can't talk.

THE WORD OF GOD

As I swing the front door open, two middle-
aged women hand me the Word of God.
I think *slam*, but can't lift

my hand, so listen, try to hear the *boom*
inside the whisper. *Would you like to know
the Lord?* and I wonder where he lives, perhaps

the mystery house at the end of the street,
or the basement apartment beyond the shared
laundry room. *I'd like that very much.*

Turns out the Lord is already inside me.
Ah, that Lord, the one who's been sniffing
at my tail of faults since I was too young

to tell the difference between stalker
and saviour. *I knew him years ago,
but we no longer talk.* Their eyes blink

like dimes at the bottom of a fountain. I want
so much to make them happy, make them moan
the way the devil would if he could, if they wanted.

The door shuts between us like solid bone,
a darkness only God can see through, his
eyes blown from the same transparency as a cat's.

THE EXPLAINED WORLD

The day dares you to pop
a few acorns in your mouth,
shut up for a minute, and crunch.

You throw your arms around
the beefy oak, bark hard
as petrified muscle. Then
a soft-needled pine, smidgens
of cone darkening your hair.
You spend ages on your knees,
foraging through moss
for a key dropped so long ago
it's become a myth.

A thicket of horsetail prehistory.
Rose quartz poking its lichen-crowned
head into a blink of wild sun.
Woodpecker hole the size of your thumb.
When you step through the space
between Siamese poplars,
you leave the explained world behind.

Balancing on two shaky stones,
you veer like a dragonfly,
as if you've just caught on
to the rules of gravity.
You lean so far to the right
a stumble loosens your ankles,
a squirrel leaps, an uneaten acorn
shivers on its stem like a bell.

THE WALK HOME

Night white in its wintering,
you pass an amusement park that
looms over the highway like heaven
with all the dead looking down.
The scaffolding of a Ferris wheel –
bones rolled into endlessness.

In the distance, gas pumps glow,
neon signs cling to their facades.

AS CLOSE AS DISTANCE

Sealed in his car, radio
gnashing its high notes. The other cars
are ships and tanks, unwieldy.
Occasional man with dog, shit bag
dangling like a designer purse.
And the great everywhere else –
as close as distance can get.
Just him, thumbs hooked
in the steering wheel, hips a little
pinched. Louise Glück
in the passenger seat, condensed
to ninety pages. Knapsack
in the back: Christmas goodies
and a windup plastic bee
that whirs – the sum of him
should the world end. As a child
revving the future, he thought
he'd be a Jetson by now, cockpit
of the galaxy. But here he is,
drooling right turns over the curb.
One day he'll drive bomb-like
into the steel-shaded lake,
finish off his loneliness. Fish
curio-dancing in the headlights.

BE DRUNK

First sip has a way of loosening
knots, those clusters of nerves
nagging like bow ties, cutting off
my breath. After a good swallow
my legs shed some texture – *hushabye*.
Knuckles shoo their useless *k*'s.
From here on in it's one grand gush –
elbows turned to slush.

Be drunk, Baudelaire proclaimed,
the poet crowning. Evening bobs
on rambunctious little waves,
the bottle cradled in my arms
a conch shell, my brain well
on its way to a saint's gibberish,
surrendering my stevedore will,
my Calvinist settle.

The second glass has a bubbly
disposition, flirty, faster
than a somersault. By the third,
the couch is surfing. At four,
I'm on the floor playing Kitty-
Kitty. Can't remember five. Come
morning, daisies will be growing
from my lips, my legs squirming
two feet from my hips.
I'll be nameless, like a beast
Adam forgot to add to his scroll.

TAMPERING

They can excise your ugliness
with a canister of liquid nitrogen
and a promise not to tell.
For moles, they cut deep
as if to dig out stain itself,
covering the scar with a bandage
that looks like doll flesh. They'll tweak
your boobs, wrinkles, folds –
knives so tiny your personality
remains miraculously intact.

They're the same people who grow your lawn
that chemistry-class green.
They can lift your ego on a swizzle stick,
make you feel as vivid as a cherry.
They're with you at the dentist's, in fact
they are the dentist, his smiling tools,
Disney playing on the ceiling screen,
the assistant with her French polish.
Lie back while pain flows up the needle.
Wrap your tongue around a drench of gratitude.

THE ABCs

Arrive! Assimilate!

Bountiful: billowing
fields and batches of
aromatic blues beneath
the can-do of a crow's
careening caw.

Dead, done – well-delved, a debt
counted on the knuckles
of one drastic hand.

Endless, and then some.

Florid, all huff and
fluster,
greed machine squeezing
God until he gives.

Homing in
on the inkling
of an ideal.

Joy
to the point of justice,
keenness without
the knowledge pronounced.

Love with its loads
of lark-like lustre.

Mega! More!

Nothing less will do,
O room of open doors.

Pillory, pineapple,
pinwheel –
the quantity
queue, the quality
raving, almost religious.

Sex like the spoon
standing in a sugar bowl.

Total truth
uncanny,
the viscera
of when, what, who.

X marks the lot.

Yearn and yearn and yearn.
Zero multiplied.

MENSCH

He calls you *mensch*, a soft, saggy
word, nonetheless a compliment.
Nice, someone else agrees:
a long-licked strawberry sucker
sweet to its colour-sapped end.
How good it is to glisten,
to listen to the oiled gears
of your own name.
What a treat to bank a glow.
Mr. Good Guy, vacant apartment
with a view, let me come live with you.
Unroll the duvet, spread the butter.
It's okay not to be alone –
a small dog of honour
tied to your wrist.

COLOUR SAMPLE

1/

We are resolved to green, then grey,
the walls flipping colours. You want
drama, while I lean toward contentment.
Deeper down, we're moving together
a crucial inch: the shush of a green
living room at noon, the constant
November grey.

How to know what we'll feel two minutes
from now. Should we succumb to white,
or *linen* as it's called at Benjamin Moore?
Or just leave the faded blue, call it
robin's dying egg? You know I wouldn't
change a thing about you, especially
the green of your eyes, Chinese jade.
And the grey at my temples? Leave it
as a nest for what's next.

2/

What I really want is a colour
that will make me swoon, twenty-one again.
I want to be a drop of ceiling paint
running down the wall, messing up perfection.

I slip the samples into separate hands
then sweep them behind my back. *You choose,*
I say, your face turning the most
mysterious shade of pink.

3/

The walls look blue in evening light,
like the skin of strangers on the subway.
Blue makes the angel in the Maynard painting
more shade-like, more icy. It brings
the death out in you, your cross of veins.
It creates shadow, sharpens chins. Blue enters
the lace spaces in the curtains
without tearing. It curls around the brass
Buddha head, slips between your fingers
leaving only the slightest smudge.

And to think, we could have painted
the room red and been afraid of everything.

OUR LIVES AND NOTHING LESS

No more white asparagus or Boursin cheese
now that cash is huddling, Dow Jones
dropping like a gored matador. Cheap
Canadian beer. The latest Lucinda
downloaded illegally. Bills shrivel
in my pocket like Kleenex fingered so long
it's turned to lint. There goes Italy next summer.
Amazing how much squeezes down the drain
with a little pressure – grapes, crusts, gristle.
No more takeout three times a week,
no more Friday nights. Soon I'll have to
sell myself in Value Village.

I used to be worth a fortune, dashed hope
exclaims. My father still leaving me
his cache of anxieties, signing them over
one by one. The whole history of the dead
is wallowing in interest never paid. Our lives
and nothing less: pickpocket crows
and mean peacocks, diamonds
wriggling from gold restraints, champagne
watered down with melting ice.

On the way back from the loan shark's,
I stop at a wheat field where sooty clouds
hang like a charcoal drawing of tragedy.
I can almost touch their weight, their sag.
That pressure again, the entire sky
on the verge of a crash. I lean against
a scratchy bale, inhale the scent
of what one day could be bread, a bit

of butter the next field over, dragging
its udder through three-leaf clovers.

AS THEY POUR THE THIRTEENTH FLOOR

As they pour the thirteenth floor,
the crane swings back and forth
with its cauldron of cement.
Shelter has become big business.
We keep our eyes on the ground
to keep from tripping over
foundations that weren't there
a glance ago. What it must have
been like to witness the first
construction: a hairy mammoth
skin stretched across two hammered poles.
For the creationists:
the moment Adam
raised his arms against the rain.
Most passersby
don't realize a crane
is flying above their heads
like a mythical bird
building its equally
mythical nest. If only
we'd been wide awake when
we made our sons and daughters,
when it was our flesh reeling
across the horizon.
What a glorious sight
that must have been:
poured honey,
hip bone nestled into pelvis.

THE TURTLES PRACTICE FINITISM

The turtles practice finitism, with sleepy superiority
give themselves up to the sun on the white rocks
in Too Good Pond. The mallards take them seriously,
flapping a fury of godlessness up and down the shore.
What will we do when the end comes, *petit frisson*?
The alpha turtle extends his neck and paddles
his claws in the air, then goes back to emulating rock.
The mallards have a flying fit, barely clearing the bridge
where I stand, fully expecting to be shat upon.

Icons swear God is there in every stroke. Saint Kosmos
and Saint Damian, hardly household names, survive without
a sense of self, all glory. How dare the turtles be so
implacable, grey shells like bullet-proof chapels
where solitary praise is the weight of a moment
lasting far too long. The only creatures found
on church walls are doves and donkeys (imagine
being God's donkey!), and the occasional dragon.
There are no holy mallards, which is the real reason
pond ducks are so unsettled, splash-landing over and over.

Should I tell you once upon a time in Athens
I saw a saint who looked like me? Holy sign,
or that turtle ego again, refusing to budge, using up
the sun? I wasn't sure which to believe in,
finally took shelter in coincidence.
The mallards coast now that they're used to me,
all wing, all graceful beauty.

Ten Thousand Repetitions

1 /

In the department of daily sounds,
Lola the chihuahua dominates
the heavy April air with her yips,
the Japanese maple buds aching
for compromise. On the street beyond,
whooshing cars could kill
with the merest thump.
A robin carols what the ear
hears as major chords.
The ceiling fan overhead
slices up my breath.
Listening is a way to let the world
enter, promiscuous as the scrape
of this very pen. The gush of my wife
brushing her teeth in the bathroom,
the tick of the kitchen clock
speaking local dialect. Listen,
until sleep returns with its fleeting
deafness – listen for the right word.

2/

My headache was shoddily
put together in a Mexican factory
with slotted screws and aluminum.
Inarticulate – claptrap of
childhood groans. The manly thing
would be to lift off the top of my skull,
plunge my fingers into the goo,
untie a wire or two until the pain
collapses like a pup tent.
Every hair numb as doll's hair.
Every thought a twinge.
Sit back and wait for pain
to find another form, a kidney stone
or heart attack, something Swiss-made
and not so easily dismissed.

3 /

I open my eyes to the same shut blinds
every morning, coloured bottles
on the windowsill divided into green
and yellow slits. Blinking makes it hard
to tell the difference between an instant
replay and a second look. On dizzy days
it feels like I'm the one who slants.

4/

A sniff of the cup before coffee pours.
When I unbutton my shirt at night,
a whiff of baby's head
clings to my chest.
I wonder whether the backs
of my knees smell like pearls.
Yesterday, I sank to a crouch
for a hyacinth, a pink rubbery thing –
dowsing me with bloom.

5 /

The Nanaimo bar has a motor at its core
which makes my tongue vibrate
long after the bite has been forgotten.
My teeth feel like pears that have just
been peeled. My uvula something rawer,
still clinging to a stem. What a glorious
way to get high. There are nights
when it seems okay to put anything
in my mouth, to be that intimate and hungry.

6/

I whir when I enter the family room,
switch on the glass lamp
that used to belong to my parents.
April nights still as cold as they've ever been.
I hum along with the portable heater,
the first few bars of a dirge, my mother
sighing from the ashes of a womb
that used to be my haven. Sounds intensify
as I flip the pages of the TV guide – buzz
flutter, crinkle, sigh.
My ankle cracks as I swing it
over my right knee, percussive,
like the leg aches my father used to rub
as he told me the story of his own bones.
The mew of the cat asking if my lap
might be worth the jump; the tock
of the grandfather clock's chastisements;
the patter of rain against windows,
each drop the same note.

A Minor Accomplishment

TOY BOX 2: PRINCESS

I remember it as brittle,
my plastic princess crown, the one
Kora pleaded with me to place on my head.
I was in my forties,
had only worn pink once before, back
in the eighties, when gender got mixed up a bit –
Boy George, the Thompson Twins,
Bryan Ferry with his soft eyes.

But Kora wasn't interested in history.
Four-year-olds are too busy dressing up the moment.
She made me sit on the rug with my legs crossed,
dubbed me Princess Barry. *Are you King?*
I asked, trying to be more involved.
Of course not, I'm a girl.

I should have known I was the type
to confuse love with humiliation,
all my feelings stuck together
like a bag of jujubes left out in the sun.

She gave me a magic wand to hold,
similar enough to a sword to pass
masculine muster. Once she got over
her delight at rendering me pink
and powerless, we played a game
where I had to choose a husband,
either a Ken doll or a chewed-up teddy bear.
She married us while single-handedly
fighting off a herd of killer dinosaurs.

I loved her so much, I held my head
straight the entire time, the crown steady
as a good reputation.

LOVE – AFTER BEATRIX POTTER

Love is what doesn't fit, becomes a longing,
both tit and tat – two fingers drawing
the long ears of a rabbit. Add colour
and you've got yourself a life, a saucer
of wanderlust swimming in blue.
Stir the meadow grass with a darting tongue,
bees dotting buttercups with commas.
The romance of finally being seen. Love
starts out as an inkling, then takes a look around,
light shedding its perplexity.

Once, you knew nothing of the intoxicated heart,
just that it honked like a goose
when it wanted room.
But now it thunders through
a well-thumbed book, title blazing,
your name in a rose-bordered box.
It crests, it curtsies, it flutters –
royal edict of a repertoire. Wrens
shake like feather dusters,
minnows quake wave to wave.
Passion with its lovely tatters
where the flesh dares innocence again.

Susurrus of a brush dipped in pink,
a blush spreading across your face,
turning the page.
Love is creating itself.
Look at how one line of colour
bleeds into the rawness of another.
Feel your own lips, unruly as piglets.

Love is a grip, a flourish.
Not even a hedgehog could be more
affirming than this: you exist
in every bristle, every stroke.

SIX TOASTS TO NEGLECTED BODY PARTS

I can smell your wrist,
a violet dipped in sea,
pulse palpitating like a wave
entering a shell. Your hand
would be nothing without this twist.
There'd be no pause in your beckon,
you dab of unlocked bone.

✦

What about your nose?
Pinocchio and his stopped-
clock boner. A snowman's
carrot where a sparrow
sits to shit. It's big alright,
a punchline, but steady.
Even its shadow has
a shadow, a gangplank
where a pirate struts his gruff.

✦

Oh, baby toe, pacify me.
A wiggle that will soon
blossom into a callus
so pink and tender
my heart will snap. I want to
wrap you in a spool of silk,
keep you cozy. I want
to soak you in a kiss.

◆

Worm nestles happily
in your navel. Deeper than
even you care to go. Way back
when, God was installing Eden
and slipped. Wrinkly, rubbery,
ripply moon. Sex made of lint.

◆

Two inches left of spine central,
your Greta Garbo mole, lonely
June bug in a spill of cream.
In the mirror, it looks like
a piece of shipwrecked
Italy. Believe me, I've
tried to lick it off, but it
clings, in love with greed.

◆

I am most in thrall of
one particular pubic hair,
a kink away from gnarl,
the colour of Cheerios.
It stirs the appropriate nerves.
But I'm deathly afraid
one day it will disengage
and end up shaken from
the morning sheets, strand of
pure forgetfulness a robin
will weave into its slapdash nest.

You'd never know how much
I'd miss you, regret I didn't
plant you between my teeth.

PORTRAIT OF APHRODITE

You knew it was hell when you lay
down with someone pale and new,
pinned him to the linen sheets
like a butterfly you'd swear was
fashioned from a prince's foreskin –
woozy with him, tongue unwinding
like the wire cage on a bottle
of champagne – only to find yourself
draped in a hot flash, the nape
of your neck dripping sweat.

Remember your prime,
when climate control was all it took
to keep your shoulders dusky. You
wore a black ribbon of a bra,
your waxed bikini line steeped
in freshly crushed lavender.
It wasn't about salvation then,
just sparkle. No need for an under-
story, not with a body composed
of countless pairs of lips.

When want becomes need, flesh
has a tendency to droop, the goosebumps
of your nipples as tempting
as bubble wrap. You try the Personals,
the dating blogs, the blinded bars,
discover that men are lying
to both themselves and you.

Hooey to self-love and all that
shut-mouth stuff. Joining a convent
would make more sense, providing
Adonis still has a sense of humour.
You finally settle for cheap stunts,
like posing nude at Sibbald Point,
Ms. October, bum jutting over the beach.

Did a man ever write a poem
for you before? I mean
other than for the way
you squished peach-like between his fingers,
the deep dive from cleavage to thighs,
the way your right thumb thrummed his tautness
to the buzz of a Hydro wire?

THE BACK SEAT

I sit in the back seat beside a pile of posters
that should have been hung weeks ago
and a *Chatelaine* proclaiming guidelines
to great sex, which makes me wonder
how many people will read this article alone
and fret. In front, husband and wife talk
about the Six Nations, but can only
remember five. How much effort
harmony takes amidst the sighs of brakes
and haunt of names like Mohawk and Seneca.

I wonder whether any single creature
stowed away on Noah's ark, an unrecorded
beast that took the world with it when it died.
Bachelor brother, castrato –
a thief who stole only from himself.
Returning home, my cat pretends
to greet me, but is really checking
for new smells. In a while we'll watch
Nicole Kidman together,
one of the dozens of her for rent.

SWALLOWS

I decide to call them swallows,
liking how far out my lips go,
and then the reprieve, that *o* sound
an actual swallow might make
as it tightens its wings.
A swarm of them, not just a flock – lassos
flinging themselves on distance.

The last time I fell in love it truly
felt like falling. One minute I was
throwing myself at the breeze,
the next landing so hard
even bone caved in. I lay there
shattered, tracking the sky
for explanations, swallowing
endless amounts of grief. Eventually,
I couldn't tell the difference between
a bird and the word. I wanted
to call it something extravagant
like *disenchantment* or *self-destruction*,
but settled on *thud* instead.

RUNDLE LOUNGE

If in the middle of a conversation
I suddenly turn, it will take nothing away

from your beauty here in the Rundle Lounge
of the Banff Springs Hotel, sipping whiskey sours,

chatting about P. K. Page and her surprise
that I wasn't short and dark, as my poems

apparently are. That damn scenery again, peaks
turning pink in the sunset, elk trimming

the lawns. If my palm lifts from your knee
don't think your bones aren't lovely, it's only

sky wanting a hand with the moon,
a pair of nimble fingers pulling threads

from the river's shined-bright rush.
If for some reason my toes stop toying

with your ankle, reproach all this rock.
If I lift my mouth from the dampness

of your neck, believe me,
once the bears have gone to bed

and the stars have fallen
you'll have me nerves and all.

FULL OF FLAME

A red glass paperweight the shape of a heart
sits on a leafy stack of love poems –
truly, only, ever.

I didn't really earn them; the words
arranged themselves rather functionally,
the way arms and legs do during sex.

If it wasn't for the dare to describe
what nipples taste like, or her pointer finger
after she's touched herself,

they'd be songs instead of poems,
canaries with cuttlebone hearts bared,
tail feathers bristling. Remember

what it felt like to be sixteen
and in love with someone you'd met
briefly in a magazine, how glossy

paper lips tasted like cucumbers
you'd later lay across your eyes
to dull the throb. I'd give one

of my lives to feel that lust again,
the ache at the centre of the earth
where rocks are full of flame.

Ha! to mere marrow and sinew
and needs that dissolve
a moment after being met.

THE WIDOW

The widow wears a flowered dress
like a silk scarf settling
on a lampshade, dimming the bulb
just a little. She misses his
subtlety, fingers warm on
her wrist. Remembers how
easily his eyes would find
those fractions of an inch
separating threads. When
she smiles, she can feel his palm
cupping her chin. The folds of hair
behind her ears, so heavy.

In accordance with the rules
of afterlife, she can't
fathom absence at all.
She can smell his thoughts –
they draw her in a direction
opposite to flesh. Her palms
are folded into shelter.

Unmussed forevermore,
she's struck by the redness
of her nipples – depth and tone
sentenced to the mirror's reversal.
Her dress lies across a cluttered
chair, lacking presence on its own.
She has no wrists tonight; his lips
are nowhere a kiss can go.

WHITEOUTS

Whiteouts on the shoulderless highway
take on the blurry swirl of you. The snow has grit,
peppers the windshield with a pesky clatter.
My car doesn't know whether to swerve or steady,
stoned from keeping its high beams trained
on the dotted white line, that flimsy border
between straight ahead and the brute unknown.
You are somewhere in the thick of my panic.
It's not that you wish me harm, just second thoughts,
a regret perhaps. By the time the sun has torched
the squalls, returning the day to extroverted schemes,
you are nowhere to be seen. The curves
look lonely, the way the roundness of a goblet
envelops itself in emptiness. I miss the old telephone
poles, the ramshackle gas stations, the hitchhikers
with their forte of small talk. I long for the next
whiteout, a great haze where I can imagine
your confusion – a minor accomplishment. States
of almost-being I somehow fooled myself meant love.

SPIDER

Your resolve to leave
had grasshopper's legs
and catapulted you
several body lengths
in one jump. In a matter
of days, you were nipping
past disgrace and heartache
as if they were truck stops
on the Trans-Canada.
Too busy leaping
to feel anything but high.

I'm more the spider type,
elaborate mandala,
so hungry I could
eat my weight in wings.
Watch me turn a monk's cell
into bitter arithmetic.
Loving me was cramped,
everything cornered.
How I miss the infinite
twisting of you.

LOVE'S BODY

Snipping toenails on the back step,
clippings scattered amidst blades of grass.
Wren cocks its head, pecks
at a shard the way it would a worm –
ninja with a dagger between his teeth.

Did Rumi ever lay a strand
of Shams' hair across his tongue?
Is it lustful to nibble on a lover's lips?

Tonight I watch a woman I've never
met before flex her turquoise
toenails. God or just distraction?
Is there a difference? Rumi would if
Rumi could. It's all true love's body.

Death Notices

ROTHKO

We talk about the black dog
that spills its breath over us –
digs a sinkhole in our brains
where runoff festers.
How could it happen to us,
cheery beings – you
with your apple-bite smile,
me with my childish fingers?
Mark Rothko orange,
a 1951 print hanging
in a doctor's office.
Blocks of suicidal thoughts.
I stare until the air
is glowing. Who knew colour
could be so heartless?
Misery grows on trees, fat
globes of negativity,
the spiked citrus stink
of sugar stirred with bile.

MOTHER ASH

for Isabelle Saunders 1919–2007

She's drifty at first, lack
of oxygen, her colouring
like kindergarten paste, her fingers
slip knots loosening on the sheets,
shrugging off her bones the way
a slip's strap slides down a shoulder.
It isn't exactly a tunnel of light,
but a narrowing nonetheless,
a button frayed to its final thread.

◆

The way she used to hold her fingers
in the air – *ta-dah* – rings winking,
bracelets spinning to her elbows.
The long vase-like shape
of her ankles. She took such care,
each step a pose, each story a legend –
back when she made the bird sing
at badminton, when the right horse
won, when she cast a shadow
on the movie screen
from her seat in the front row.

◆

What would she have pictured
when she thought of ash?

Maybe a cigarette
Hedy Lamarr had just taken
from her sex-red mouth, a soft,
silver centipede clinging
for dear life. Or the smudge
of a cross on Jennifer Jones'
holy forehead. Death was nothing new,
just longer than the previews.

✦

She arrives home in a golden brown urn
less regal than a limousine.
It's all real now, the black plastic bag
almost incandescent, the shocking heft,
her name hand-printed and the word
remains, as in *lingers*.

✦

Refusing to settle, we put photos of her
on the mantel, near the TV set.
The room's colours complement
her hair, red as that cushion from Spain.
And when the TV's off, it can double
as a big-screen mirror.

✦

Flowers ring the doorbell, sympathy
bouquets. She kept the irises
at her side, but placed the roses
dead centre, dining room table,

gazing up at the chandelier.
She could have sat all day and stared.
Carnations the most solicitous,
their frills like secret pockets.

All these feelings rising up such skinny stems.

✦

Her astrological chart tucked
in a drawer, those twelve cold houses
where destiny defies logic.
When she was born, fate hung on
to Aries with the babiest of veins.
For awhile, Leo rising explained it all.
Moon on top of her
soaked in rocket fuel.

✦

It's snowing in the galaxy tonight,
or is that her ghost wearing someone
else's glasses? Planets blur,
confused with stars. Such a long way
for loss to travel, but it does.
It's snowing everywhere – in the inside
pockets of our coats.

DANGLING

We'll do this daily if we have to,
even if it takes all winter. And so
I watch her search, having pledged
not to lose her too when we both
stood beside the great white bed
of her mother's passing.
Everything gleams to distraction.
A chunk of tire-ice wears its shine
like a rhinestone. I try to help
but my new glasses make even
the familiar strange. Since these
are the earrings she bought
when her mother lay dying
in that glorious autumn of a hospital,
it's a double loss. She left
the house, silver earrings swaying,
but by the time she brushed snow
from the car, coat collar scraping
against her ears, one of the dangles
had dropped into a drift, hidden by
the tiny flurry of its impact.

DEATH NOTICES

1/ SWEET DROWNING — AFTER YEATS

The boat, a barge with a shilling's worth
of profile, sailed into the harbour
like a whale out for a moonlight soak.
Nothing in the realm, not even
a blackbird glaring north. Round
went the helm, a tidy groan of steel,
dock deep-notched and unforgiving. Yet
he could fathom it all again,
                    will,
follow waves and mermaid tails. He
could voyage to the very end, those
icicle seas, that starlit staircase
where angels have collapsed. Mostly, midst,
he has lived this life (*good godhood!*)
boldly, up to his thighs in chill.
Too sudden a spill, it couldn't have
been helped. Sail all the way to hell,
gripping the mast, tenacious as a monkey.

2/ SWEET REVENGE – AFTER PLATH

A frog-shaped German tank steams trenches in the mud,
impermeable; I can feel it in the hard-quartz heart of me.
I have made sure my legacy has crush and aim –
even kittens have turned to tread.
Who'd want a memory so light it blew away?
I want the weight of his body on mine, eternal pain.
Vice versa, croaked the crow. Yes, yes. Every last word
flattened like a fossil. Take down the hills, dredge the
riverbeds, roll over the roses until each thorn
has softened its grasp. Then let me lie in the ditch,
scalded, one-dimensional. Just try to kiss
these squashed hands – bitter bride, empty nest.

3/ SWEET TRANSFORMATION – AFTER WHITMAN

The feeble/glorious arms of men,
handing burdens over,
passing on, away. Muscle is the
soul sprung to life, the
secret vice, the hard seed in the crux
of the sunflower.
I rest my cheek on a bicep: Jacob
and his stone pillow.
The cool crook of an elbow
cradles me like a womb, a room
where I can twist the sheets
and almost die.
It's the last man who'll
carry me the farthest, whose
flesh I leave my own flesh to.
Let us both burst into sweat,
let us rain flames on grief
and smoke ourselves a dark new
glory. A blindness jarring.
Just one more step, one
more embrace. When you leave
my body at the door, both skin
and bone become the painted wood,
the blue, the hinge, the knob
that revolves around the sun.

4 / SWEET OBLIVION – AFTER SEXTON

It's a red convertible, no doubt,
sleek chrome bumpers, whitewalls,
horn that wails like a woman
making love for the third time
in one luscious night. Skid marks
in the suburbs, *pish*, smoke rings
lapping at the rear view mirror.
Thirty miles to the gallon,
cruise control, a radio
Nat King Cole calls home.
Watch the curb crumble
when you pull away bleeding
internally from a dozen
different wounds. Feel the way
speed turns your heart inside out.
Next stop NYC, Broadway torn into
little glittery pieces.
Going so far and fast, the poem
can't hold on to a single word,
naked as the road's shoulder, as
those split white lines running down
the middle of every distance.
You could take a ride with God
in this, watch his head blow off
as you break the scream barrier.

POSITIVITY

I pass a cemetery selling *Graves & Niches*
on my way to the beach, and claustrophobia
settles in. I try to walk it off, forcing
the sun to magnify my shadow. At the empty
lifeguard station, I realize that being prepared
for the worst is a negative thought. It's the deep-down
things that kill us. Better to fill myself
with a dyed orchid of a sky. Dogs snuffling
across the sand like mechanical shovels,
lovers slapping volleyballs back and forth.
Beneath layers of socks and shoes, my toes
are ready to be reborn. At my core,
waves sweep pebbles into temporary walls.

MILTON'S GRAVE

Milton lay in his Cripplegate grave
repeating to himself that one blindness
was similar to another. He felt the weight
of time-to-come the way he'd once borne sky.
This was no more alone than his wives' deaths
had made him feel. As he'd feared, paradise
had nothing to do with him.
Still, there was comfort: no more
ink-starved pens, no tasks waiting
like supplicants by his bedside.

When the digging started again, he wondered
if he might be taken for a stroll,
perhaps to the oak leaning over the river.
Without eyes or faith, journeys were nothing
but vibration. He heard the scrape
of the coffin lid lifted, raindrops thumping
lightly on his chest. So this is the afterlife,
he mused, the breath of his intruder
sour with something undercooked.
He didn't like the feeling of being watched
but couldn't do a thing about it.

The ugly crack of bones breaking
turned out to be the only sound he could make.
In pieces, there was more of him.
His wrist popped out like an owl's egg,
though his femur had to be wrenched.
His baby finger would make a fine
conversation piece. And his teeth,
raw and slimy as ruined souls.

By the time the robber
had filled her corset with silver,
Milton was almost boneless.
Like a saint, he thought, as if his Catholic
heritage had tracked him down.
Like a snake condemned never to
lift its belly off the ground.
Where was God in all this meddling?
What they buried a second time
could hardly be called a man.

SLAUGHTER

In the back of the Hunter's Meat truck
pigs full of grain and penicillin hang from hooks
embedded between their shoulder blades.
They swing a little in the tar and diesel breeze,
pastry pink, too naive to feel shame or descend
into grief, just hanging there sleek and vulnerable
as if the worst hadn't already happened, as if
they were waiting to be released, their dark hooves
eager to scamper across the parking lot,
into the Chinese restaurant where they'll be
sliced and barbecued, an *mmm* on the shiny lips
of a hungry man who might as well be me.

Then the orange rose on Maureen's
dining room table, in the Brierley crystal vase
she won for a love poem; it's still doing
a slight soft-shoe, and smells like my mother
used to behind her ears. You'd never guess
it was dying – in fact inserted between the clipped
teeth of one of those pigs, it would almost
constitute a resurrection. Squeals deep
in my cochlea like dirty needles.

Dreaming wide that night, territorial as any beast,
I'm piglike in only the best of ways, thriving
in a fantasy where all the orange roses have been
shorn of thorns, feeding on fallen petals,
an essential part of an ecosystem that doesn't
include slaughter. So when the farmer appears
we make love instead of blood, pink on pink,
surprisingly clean for two such fervent animals.

WHITE PANSY, 1927 — GEORGIA O'KEEFFE

It's like those photos of the dead,
disengaged in some essential way,
but beautiful, an innerness
so intent the wall glows. The spot
where soul once came and went, the only
real colour, yolk-gold, though mauve-black
bruises mar the pinched fringe. The rest white,
glacial cheeks and chin. Why didn't
she place it in a vase? Memory
alone doesn't keep
anything alive. All that's left
is the levitating smell of oil,
the shush of a hog's hair brush.
A flower long gone, petals crisp
and cold, puckered at the core
like lips sewn shut.

What is art?

A gasp.
Life staring you down
with its bone face.

POSTCARD FROM LORCA, AUGUST 1936

The black fig trees at Huerta de San Vicente
suggested I write to you, begging you to care
for them, not me, so they might have eyes to see,
visions to scatter on the stony ground.
The world must be coaxed to stay alive now
that even words have infusible hearts. Who
but a poet will sip the sacrifice
oozing from sliced stems and curls of peeled bark?
Holiness, like sex, leaves a lonely blood
on the shine of so much loss.

Here is a picture of what I might have become
had my trembling wrists been tied with roots instead of rope.

McMICHAEL GALLERY, AFTER HOURS

October leaves smeared onto branches
like sticky drops of jam. Sketches
with their pentimenti. Harris looming
inside his mountains. Lismer
leaning like frail ballet. And Thomson
so tangled up in Algonquin Park,
his canoe capsizes. Everything-
but-the-kitchen-sink waterfalls.
What used to be wild – clouds
dabbed into place. Dead of night:
west wind blows, brush strokes billow.
Giant windowpanes rattle in their frames.

AMY WINEHOUSE

She winks her way
through the rehab song,
pleasure blips like red poppies
crushed in the creases of her brain.

The cognitive is every bit
as much a mystery as the soulful
way she stands here whacked and wary,
fidgety fingers ravelling knots,
her voice the crack within a crack.

Like Billie when her cheeks
were going grey, a wilted
gardenia of an eyelid.

She sings about being stoned,
groped and dropped, overhanded
by love in all its surliness.
As if a soft-shelled egg is tucked
beneath her chin. Is this what's meant
by *broken*?

What does she think she is: the spray
at the tip of a needle?

THE WEEPING MONKEY — AFTER JULIE OAKES

Why do you cry? I ask
the weeping monkey. Unhappiness
is the human condition. His tears have
almost worn fur and flesh to bone,
as if grief were a kind of alchemy.
He curls into his pain, tail a slack piece of rope.

How blind he must be behind all
these tears, higher branches indistinct.
No difference between an anthill
and a lion. Drop by drop, encased,
embraced, his sobs dig trenches
in whatever's tender.

The monkey and I hunker down,
our shared misery like two grey pearls
in one shell. It's good to feel
the bristle of his wet face, press my features
into his. We weep a path that leads us
deeper than the will to stay afloat.

Disturbing the Buddha

1/ PSALM 19

The heavens declare God's grandeur:
cloud trains, fire-breathing horizons
and the colour yellow just floating there
amidst a wash of blue. Your job
is to crane your neck, origami muscle,
strain your eyes to make the distinction
between a check mark and a plane.
Your mission is to rename
the planets, something far outside
the alphabet and numbers
with their built-in greed. Say nothing
to the angels who think they're egrets,
or the parachutes that fall
like divas. Ignore the water-
colour dye jobs, the pencil
signatures at the horizon,
the sour face pasted on the moon.
Grandeur is a kind of nothingness,
illusion and its lack
of oxygen. A dazzle of ice-pick
holes, light desperate to breathe.

2 / LAO-TZU

A good traveller has no fixed plans,
no reservations, no guest room
at the end of Aunt Lillian's
ivory hall. The road is leaky
fate, a suet ball and a slow beak.
You walk on an early version
of legs, tumble where the hills grow
chins, follow your nose for wild
lilacs and china cups of rain.
If a street lamp throws you a zinger,
duck west. If love grabs you by the short-
term memory, retrace your steps.
Up or down, no matter. Heaven
is a still life in a Motel Six
non-smoker. You can get there on thumbs
alone. Believe in somersaults,
in flagging down a fleet of cabs,
in hoisting yourself out of dried-up
wells, let it happen. Tonight
you'll sleep in a clearing
that won't be there come dawn.

3 / SENG-TS'AN

The Great Way isn't difficult,
it's spread in the webs of your fingers
and toes. It's that first cinder of ash,
that hiccup as the grapefruit takes
to the spoon, that dream of being chased
across the Gotham skyline. Knowing
what to do, there's the hard part, how
diagram A connects to the picture
on the box, the rosy outcome of patience.
Only the willing bits fit. The rest
is resistance, an odds and ends drawer.
Dare you pull yourself into a crouch,
life unfolding in all directions?
Breathe in through your forehead, the extra
hole that never closes. See your
elbow blink, your right thigh reach for
the car keys. Who cares which
foot disappears first? The Great Way
will find you, fingers waving from your groin.

4 / KŪKAI

A hand moves, and the fire's whirling
takes different shapes: elephant ears,
umbrellas. An eyebrow turns
into the handle on a mug. A wink,
the cavity in a front tooth. Even a fuck
is deceptive, wet wind whistling
down a bamboo shoot. You never know
when a cockroach will spring into
a dragon, when the mirror hangs on
the verge of truth. Never know when
death is just a decoy. A knee moves
and a bicycle wheel becomes
the hurried sun, spokes dividing
light into bracelets on a
disembodied wrist. Transformation
is how God began, idea/
delusion, a list of all the things
you wish made sense. One minute
the anchor of a question mark,
the next a blur of mud.

5 / WU-MEN

The Great Way has no gate,
no buzzer, no knob, no
iron bars that only breath
can penetrate. It's an entry
wound, skin pushed to the limits,
like the Red Sea's shores. Look
at all the traffic – swallows
hugging their speed, cruise ships
shaking their Jell-O-green pools,
genies shooting
skateboard flares. One toe at a time
and you're through, propelled by
desire's tiniest thrust. One
juicy thought and your consciousness
explodes. It's where your loneliness
was already heading,
where stamps have been flying
on perforated wings. Forget
the foolishness of choice.
You haven't had an unconflicted thought
since your mother's breast morphed
into a plastic Goofy cup.
You knew then and there, fate
was an openness to
folly. The Buddha so
disturbed, his belly rolled
across the lawn like a
freshly fallen orange.

6 / RUMI

Forget your life. Say God is Great. *Get up.*
Pour yourself a glass of silver tongues. Slice
the pages of your favourite diary.
Send the roosters off to rooster school.
When all the floods are wearing ties,
preferably Windsor knots, and the fireflies
are playing dominoes, take
a minute to exchange your flesh
for jewels, to make humility glow.
No good just lying there
in gilded picture frames. Life
is so much more than walking on your thumbs.
It's time to rinse the envies, rearrange
the syllables. Gobbledygook,
a synonym for praise, a call to
action. The only way to worship
is with all three hands. Get up. Hang
the paint cans. Twirl the twigs until even
the oaks are flying. Grab a piece of
God and feed the anarchy of joining in.

7 / MECHTHILD OF MAGDEBURG

Of all that God has shown me,
you say, pointing at the fig juice
trickling down the blonde man's chin,
at the crow sitting on the army-
green garbage can as if it were
a golden egg, at the distortion
of the young girl's ankles in the
Camry's hubcap. Your finger points
for such a long time, turning into
a telescope with its own visions
of the galaxy's pores and cracks.
All the way to doubt and back, the source
where trust begins to wrinkle, the
moment when a nerve's pleasure
veers toward pain. You can't stop pointing
at the blonde man's drool.
It's a wonder that crow doesn't
snap your finger like a cracker.
How dare you list all the garbage
within. These are your eyeballs' sins.
All the things God made when he was
desperate to be noticed.

8 / KABIR

Student, do the simple purification.
Dump your purse on the welcome mat.
Slip off the leather straps of your
shoes. Roll down your sleeves until they swallow
your hands. Unwind your belt until
it becomes a whip again, lose the need
to hold so much in. Drop your jeans and
underpants, your sex huge as the X
on a treasure map. Shimmy away from
it like a snake's coil of shed skin, embrace
the blank. Unhook your ribs, abandon
the myth of your gender. Screw off
your head, your lips collapsing like
a badly translated French kiss.
Shuck your soul, strip it of its many
lifetimes, leave it on the back of
the kitchen door like an apron
no one will ever wear. Not even
words can fix you anymore.

9 / GENSEI

Trailing my stick I go down to the garden edge
where the wilderness has drawn
a thick line of weeds, where snakes writhe freely
like teenage boys, and innocence is eaten
organs and all. Where the idea of you
finally makes no sense, quicksand sucking on
emptiness. Are you able to watch your
body disappear? You step into moss
and the sharpness of your heels sinks,
branches close in above you like lace
woven from sap. A dragonfly perches
on your left ear. A cluster of sumac flares.
The stick falls from your usually stubborn fist
and suddenly you're undergrowth.
It won't be long before the deer
are nibbling you, silent over your sweetness,
tongues soft as those childhood prayers
you thought had gone to heaven long ago.
You'll have to rethink your notion of afterlife
once the deer have licked you to the bone.

10 / RYŌKAN

First days of spring – the sky
a slice of blue pie, horizons
tied into bows of ivory cloud.
There are all kinds of death out there,
in here, but you are busy
weighing choices: bulb or seed,
womb or dirt. You are preparing
the ingredients for an auto-
biography, paring knives
twinkling, plenty of warm
water. A swaddle of fresh
skin, a milky molecule.
The perfect detail of
a new name. But until then
you prefer referring to your
lack of self as consequence
instead of fate. Back to the idea
of an idea, when metaphor
was still called myth. For now
it's wise to stop disturbing the Buddha,
let him catch up on his mysteries.
Spring sits cross-legged on a mountain
of ploughed snow, slowly
descending to solid ground.

ACKNOWLEDGEMENTS

Poems from this collection have been published in the following journals: *Canadian Poetries* ("The ABCs," "Toy Box," "The Word of God," and "The Explained World"); *Eighteen Bridges* ("White Peony, 1927 – Georgia O'Keeffe" and "Our Lives and Nothing Less"); *The Fiddlehead* ("Portrait of Aphrodite" and "Rundle Lounge"); *The Malahat Review* ("As Close as Distance"); *Prairie Fire*, as 3rd place winner in the Banff Centre Bliss Carman Poetry Award Contest ("Ten Thousand Repetitions"); *The Winnipeg Review* ("Spider" and "Be Drunk").

The "Disturbing the Buddha" section was published as a chapbook by The Alfred Gustav Press, Series Six, 2011. The first line of each of these poems comes from the book *The Enlightened Heart: An Anthology of Sacred Poetry*, edited by Stephen Mitchell (HarperPerennial, 1989). The inspiration first arrived from Julie Oakes' installation Buddha Composed at the Varley Gallery in Markham, Ontario in 2008.

Even if I repeated my gratitude ten thousand times, it still wouldn't be enough to show my appreciation for the support of Brick Books and all its wonders. Sue Sinclair was a dream editor, contributing to both the intricacies and the vision behind these poems with tenderness and precision. Once again, Alayna Munce turned copy-editing into an art. And Kitty Lewis tended to everything else with great warmth and joy.

Much appreciation to Karen Dempster, my partner in poems and all things real. And to my writing groups who are invaluable in how well they always listen to what it is I mean to say.

BARRY DEMPSTER, twice nominated for the Governor General's Award, is the author of fourteen poetry collections. His collection *The Burning Alphabet* won the Canadian Authors' Association Chalmers Award for Poetry in 2005. In 2010 and again in 2015, he was a finalist for the Ontario Premiers Award for Excellence in the Arts, and in 2014 he was nominated for the Trillium Award for his novel *The Outside World*. He lives in Holland Landing, Ontario.